12/93

Dear Aunt Margie
        Merry Chri~~~~

Agatha is very ~~~~
have the warmth ~~~~
care that you ha~~~ given her!
I know she will bring you all
the joy and love!
        Happy New Year! I Love
You very much!

                Shelly

LESLEY ANNE IVORY'S

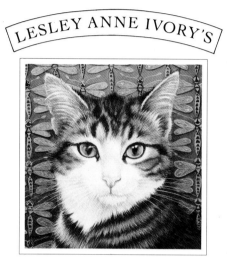

~ PERFECT ~ LITTLE CATS

Crown Publishers, Inc. New York

Here by the sacred hearth I lie,
High priest of the silken mat,
Guarding with imperious eye
   The precinct of the cat.

This vigil is a solemn trust -
I know so many things you don't.
I'm doing it because I must,
   And I know you won't.

JAMES WESTON, 'THE SENTINEL'

The cat is domestic only as far as suits its own ends; it will not be kennelled or harnessed nor suffer any dictation as to its goings out or comings in. Long contact with the human race has developed in it the art of diplomacy, and no Roman Cardinal of medieval days knew better how to ingratiate himself with his surroundings than a cat with a saucer of cream on its mental horizon.

SAKI (HECTOR HUGH MUNRO), *THE ACHIEVEMENT OF THE CAT*

A female cat is kept young in spirit and supple in body by the restless vivacity of her kittens. She plays with her little ones, fondles them, pursues them if they roam too far, and corrects them sharply for all the faults to which feline infancy is heir. A kitten dislikes being washed quite as much as a child does, especially in the neighbourhood of its ears. It tries to escape the infliction, rolls away, paddles with its little paws, and behaves as naughtily as it knows how, until a smart slap brings it suddenly back to subjection.

AGNES REPPLIER, *THE FIRESIDE SPHINX*

You all day long, beside the fire,
Retrace in dreams your dark desire,
And mournfully complain
In grave displeasure, if I raise
Your languid form to pat or praise;
And so to sleep again.

You loved me when the fire was warm,
But, now I stretch a fondling arm,
You eye me and depart.
Cold eyes, sleek skin, and velvet paws,
You win my indolent applause,
You do not win my heart.

ARTHUR BENSON, 'THE CAT'

Come, lovely cat, and rest upon my heart,
And let my gaze dive in the cold
Live pools of thine enchanted eyes that dart
Metallic rays of green and gold.

CHARLES BAUDELAIRE, *LES FLEURS DU MAL*

The love of dress is very marked in this attractive animal; he is proud of the lustre of his coat, and cannot endure that a hair of it shall lie the wrong way. When the cat has eaten, he passes his tongue several times over both sides of his jaws, and his whiskers, in order to clean them thoroughly; he keeps his coat clean with a prickly tongue which fulfils the office of the curry-comb.

CHAMPFLEURY (JULES HUSSON), *THE CAT PAST AND PRESENT*

When she so carefully avoids the glasses on the dinner-table she is not thinking of her behaviour as a dependent of civilized man, but acting in obedience to hereditary habits of caution in the stealthy chase, which is the natural accomplishment of her species. She will stir no branch of a shrub lest her fated bird escape her, and her feet are noiseless that the mouse may not know of her coming.

P. G. HAMMERTON, *CHAPTERS ON ANIMALS*

When with delicate blandishments we have beguiled a cat from her reserve, when she responds, coyly at first, and then with graceful abandon to our advances, when the soft fur brushes our cheek, when the gleaming eyes narrow sleepily, and the murmurous purr betrays the sweetness of her content, we feel like a lover who has warily and with infinite precaution stolen from his capricious mistress the first tender token of possible surrender.

AGNES REPPLIER, *THE FIRESIDE SPHINX*

Cats are of a loving nature, and delight in displaying it towards those whom they select for attention; they rub against them, or insist on being nursed, purring loudly and continuously the while. Frequently they exhibit a decidedly jealous tendency, and resent notice taken by their owners of other cats. Indeed, there is an anecdote told of one puss who, if displeased, marked her disapprobation by deliberately taking a distant seat and turning her back to the company.

ANNE MARKS, *THE CAT IN HISTORY, LEGEND, AND ART*

He's delicately tough, endearingly reserved,
Adaptable, fastidious, rope-and-fibre-nerved.
Now an accomplished Yogi, good at sitting still,
He ponders ancient mysteries on the window-sill,
Now stretches, bares his claws and saunters off to find
The thrills of love and hunting, cunningly combined.
Acrobat, diplomat, and simple tabby cat,
He conjures tangled forests in a furnished flat.

MICHAEL HAMBURGER, 'LONDON TOM-CAT'

The cat, it is well to remember, remains the friend of man because it pleases him to do so and not because he must. Resourceful, brave, intelligent (the brain of a kitten is comparatively larger than that of a child), the cat is in no sense a dependent and can revert to the wild state with less readjustment of values than any other domestic animal.

CARL VAN VECHTEN, *THE TIGER IN THE HOUSE*

The tortoiseshell cat
She sits on the mat
As gay as a sunflower she;
In orange and black you see her blink,
And her waistcoat's white, and her nose is pink,
And her eyes are green as the sea.
But all is vanity, all the way;
Twilight's coming, and close of day,
And every cat in the twilight's grey,
Every possible cat.

PATRICK R. CHALMERS, 'THE TORTOISESHELL CAT'

He ate when he was hungry, slept when he was sleepy, and enjoyed existence to the very tips of his toes and the end of his expressive and slow-moving tail. He delighted to roam about the garden and stroll among the trees, and to lie on the green grass and luxuriate in all the sweet influences of summer.

CHARLES DUDLEY WARNER, *MY SUMMER IN A GARDEN*

He settles down as close to me as possible, after stretching out his paw towards me two or three times, looking at me as though craving permission to leap on to my knees. And there he lies, his head daintily resting on my arm, as though to say: 'Since you will not have me altogether, permit this at least, for I shall not disturb you if I remain so.'

PIERRE LOTI, *REFLETS SUR LA ROUTE SOMBRE*

It might almost be said that cats divine the idea which descends from the brain to the tip of the pen, and that, stretching out their paws, they wish to seize it in its passage. They like silence, order, and quietness, and no place is so proper for them as the study of a man of letters ... I should add that among the pretty creatures, so pleasant by day, there is a nocturnal side, mysterious and cabalistic, which is very seductive to the poet.

THÉOPHILE GAUTIER, PREFACE TO CHARLES BAUDELAIRE'S
LES FLEURS DU MAL

Copyright © 1992 by Russell Ash and Bernard Higton
Illustrations copyright © 1992 by Lesley Anne Ivory
Licensed by Copyrights

Published by Crown Publishers, Inc.,
201 East 50th Street, New York, New York 10022.
Member of the Crown Publishing Group.

Originally published in Great Britain by
Pavilion Books Limited in 1992.

Manufactured in Singapore

Library of Congress Cataloging-in-Publication Data

Ivory, Lesley Anne.
  Lesley Anne Ivory's perfect little cats.
    p.   cm.
  1. Ivory, Lesley Anne. 2. Cats in art. I. Title.
II. Title: Perfect little cats.
ND497.I86A4 1992   92-3340
159. 2–dc20   CIP

ISBN 0-517-59103-0

10 9 8 7 6 5 4 3 2 1

First American Edition

Text extracts from the following sources are reprinted with the kind permission of the publisher
and copyright holders stated. Should any copyright holder have been inadvertently
omitted they should apply to the publishers who will credit them in full in any subsequent editions:
Patrick R. Chalmers, 'The Tortoiseshell Cat' from A Peck O'Maut, Methuen;
Michael Hamburger for extract from 'London Tom Cat';
Carl van Vechten, extract from The Tiger in the House, Heinemann 1921, Alfred Knopf, 1924.